Fort Point

Sentry at the Golden Gate

by

JOHN A. MARTINI

Contents

The Golden Gate National Park Association is a non-profit membership organization established to support the education, conservation and research programs of the Golden Gate National Recreation Area.

PUBLISHED BY
GOLDEN GATE NATIONAL
PARK ASSOCIATION

ISBN 0-9625206-5-9

It has been called "the pride of the Pacific," "the Gibraltar of the West Coast," and "one of the most perfect models of masonry in America." When construction began during the height of the California gold rush, Fort Point was planned as the most formidable deterrence America could offer to a naval attack on California. Although its guns never fired a shot in anger, Fort Point has witnessed Civil War, obsolescence, earthquake, bridge construction, remodeling for later wars, and restoration as a National Historic Site. It stands today beneath the soaring Golden Gate Bridge as a monument to more than two centuries of military presence on San Francisco Bay. The fort also bears silent and eloquent testimony to the craftsmanship of the Army engineers who designed it and the workers who erected it.

The site of Fort Point was originally a high promontory known to 18th-century Spanish colonizers as "Punta del Cantil Blanco"—White Cliff Point. Located at the narrowest part of the only entrance to San Francisco Bay, the point was an obvious location for a fort to keep out enemy ships. In 1794 the Spanish erected a tiny adobe gun battery atop Cantil Blanco as defense against possible British and Russian aggression. Christened "Castillo de San Joaquin," the little fort and its handful of century-old bronze and iron guns soon fell victim to the harsh San Francisco climate. Adobe walls melted in the rain, and lack of repair funds from far-off Madrid led to eventual ruin of the Castillo. Shortly after Mexico gained its independence from Spain in 1821, the fort was abandoned to the elements.

The only invasion in San Francisco's history occurred at the Castillo in 1846 during the short-lived "Bear Flag Revolt."

Early in the morning of July 1, a rough-hewn group of Yankees, led by John Charles Fremont and Kit Carson began the long pull across the Bay from Sausalito to the ancient Spanish fort "Castillo de San Joaquin" on the San Francisco shore. They called themselves "Bear Flaggers" after their flag of revolution, and their goal was the liberation of California from Mexican control.

Nosing their launch into a sheltered cove below the fort, the raiders scrambled up the hundred-foot hillside, swarmed into the crumbling Castillo and spiked the cannon mounted within its walls. The only tarnish on the victory was that the Castillo had not been garrisoned for a dozen years. "In the absence of a garrison with no powder," wrote one caustic historian, "it is not surprising that not one of the ten cannon offered the slightest resistance."

United States military forces were shortly in control of California. The growing American population gave local landmarks new names, and the old Castillo soon became known as "Fort Blanco." The point upon which it sat was simply nicknamed "Fort Point."

It was a name that would stick.

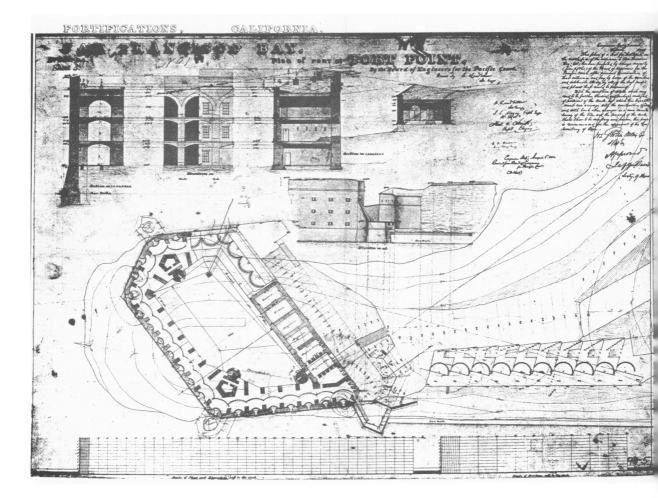

Third System Fort

Fort Point is typical of American "Third System" forts, so-called because they were the third generation of permanent forts erected by the United States to protect harbors and coasts. Nearly forty similar forts were built by the Army's Corps of Engineers along the Atlantic and Gulf coasts. The fort at Fort Point, however, would be the only casemated Third System work built on the shores of the Pacific.

A Fort to Guard the Golden Gate
1848 – 1868

THE CALIFORNIA GOLD RUSH of 1848 took the United States by surprise. Not only was the wealth of the gold fields nearly incalculable, but ship traffic into San Francisco increased dramatically. Only a few ships a year had previously visited the port, but during 1849 alone, 770 vessels entered the Golden Gate. Commerce was booming, and docks, a Navy yard and other strategic harbor installations were under construction. The military suddenly found itself responsible for protecting the most valuable prize in North America—San Francisco Bay.

While the U.S. Army quickly realized that permanent defenses were needed, it would take time to plan and build major fortifications, or "works," to protect the Bay. The harbor needed immediate security, so in March 1849, six modern artillery pieces were temporarily mounted inside the remains of the old Castillo de San Joaquin. The following year, a joint Army-Navy board convened to make recommendations for defending the entire Pacific coast. Their report, released on November 1, 1850, focused on San Francisco Bay and the Golden Gate channel as the keys to defense of the new state. The board recommended the construction of two major forts, one on either shore of the Golden Gate's straits formed by Fort Point and Lime Point. The proposed forts would provide a devastating crossfire where the channel measured little more than a mile wide, focusing the effect of several hundred cannon upon any enemy ship entering the Bay.

Backing up this outer line of defense would be an inner line centered around a third major fort on Alcatraz Island. This fort, in turn, would be backed up by smaller batteries on Angel Island, Yerba Buena Island, and Point San Jose on the northern San Francisco waterfront. Any ship making it through the crossfire at the Golden Gate would thus have to run a gauntlet of additional gun batteries no matter which course it chose through the Bay.

Board members were very insistent that work begin immediately at Fort Point, where "the first work for the defense of the passage should be placed, and nothing should be allowed to interfere with bringing this battery as rapidly as possible to a state of efficiency." They specified the fort should be "as powerful in its fire on the water as . . . the largest of our fortifications on the Atlantic," and recommended mounting over 100 cannon of the largest caliber available.

The style of fort proposed by the engineers was a massive, multi-storied masonry structure containing scores of smoothbore cannon. The guns would be mounted both in enclosed "casemates" and in open "barbette" batteries atop the fort's roof. Within its five- to seven-foot thick walls would also be quarters for the officers and soldiers, store rooms, powder magazines, and enough water and provisions to withstand a six-month siege.

Before work could begin on construction of the fort, the remains of the old Castillo and the heights of Cantil Blanco had to be leveled. Military technology of the day dictated that the lowest level of guns in the fort should be as close to the water as possible. The new work would be built at an elevation only fifteen feet above the Bay. The entire tip of the hundred-foot-high peninsula would have to be cut down nearly to sea level to provide a platform for the huge casemated fort.

By mid-September of 1853, a construction gang had demolished the old Castillo and begun leveling the promontory, spreading its rocky spoil along the base of the cliffs east and west of the point. It took a year of chipping and blasting at the serpentine rock to complete a platform measuring 150 yards by 100 yards. Once the site was cleared, work began on the massive foundations for the fort itself.

Triangular Defense of the Bay

The Army's original plan for defending San Francisco Bay envisioned three huge masonry forts that would form a triangle of converging cannon fire just inside the Golden Gate.

FINDING THE NECESSARY BUILDING materials at reasonable prices became a never-ending problem for the engineers overseeing the project. Very few of the sources of brick and stone in California met the Army's high standards for use in fortifications. Adding to the engineers' problems was the remoteness of California; every construction bid and material sample examined by the local Army engineers had to be reviewed by Chief of Engineers General Joseph Totten in Washington, D.C. During the Gold Rush, the simple act of sending a memo and receiving a reply took as long as three months.

In late 1854, the supervising engineer at Fort Point finally secured permission to use granite imported from China in the work's foundations; it was of better quality than anything he had been able to find in California, and it cost less than local stone despite being shipped over 5,000 miles. As soon as the foundation trenches were dug, workers laid the slabs of granite atop concrete footings secured to bedrock. Inside the perimeter of the foundations, additional excavations were made for five deep cisterns that would hold 200,000 gallons of water for use during time of siege.

Once the foundations were complete, construction began on the arched casemates that would provide rooms for the garrison and guns. The fort's floor plan was basically an irregularly-shaped

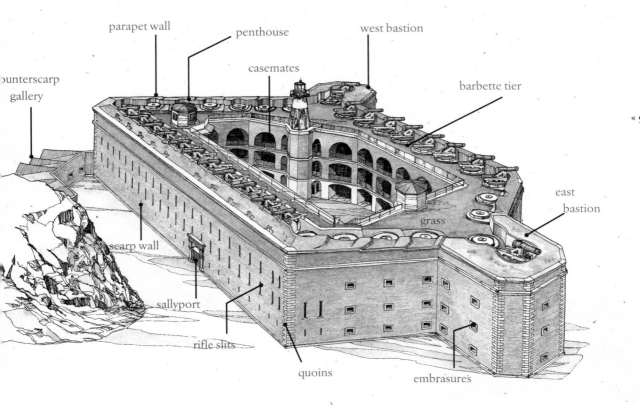

parapet wall · penthouse · west bastion · casemates · barbette tier · counterscarp gallery · east bastion · scarp wall · grass · sallyport · rifle slits · quoins · embrasures

rectangle with four principle sides, or faces. The west, north, and east faces looked out on the straits of the Golden Gate and into the harbor, and it was on these sides that the fort mounted three tiers of guns. The south side of the fort, officially known as the "gorge," would contain the powder magazines, storerooms, tiny jail, kitchens and barracks for the garrison. In the center of this land face stood the only entrance to the fort—a heavily guarded "sallyport," or protected passageway, sealed at both ends by heavy oak doors. Atop the fort was the barbette tier which mounted guns on all four sides. On the hill behind the fort, an additional ten-gun battery known as an "outwork" was planned, providing still more protection.

Three years into the project, changes were made to the original semi-rectangular outline of the fort. The engineers added two flanking towers, or "bastions," jutting out from the east and west faces of the main work, and they discarded their plan to build a moat separating the fort from the land. They also decided not to build the fort entirely of granite, even though the first tier had been partially completed. Instead, most of the fort would be constructed of brick made to the engineers' specifications in their own brickyard on the hill south of the fort.

Work progressed at a steady pace on construction of the tiers of casemates on the waterfronts and gorge face. Master masons were recruited for dressing and setting the granite blocks and laying the millions of brick required in the work. To assist them, the engineers recruited a small army of journeymen masons, carpenters, blacksmiths, teamsters, and common laborers from the swollen ranks of unemployed miners who had gone "bust" in the gold fields.

By late 1859, the fort's walls had nearly reached their full height and the work was almost ready to receive its armament. The two additional bastions brought the total number of gun positions inside the fort's walls to 126, while the outwork battery above the fort could mount ten more guns. A detached "counterscarp gallery" capable of handling an additional five guns had also been built facing the sallyport, bringing the grand total to 141 cannon positions at "the fort at Fort Point."

The Civil War Years: Occupying the Fort

Ironically, as the fort neared completion, funds grew scarce. By late 1860, the labor force had been reduced to just a few men engaged in setting flagstones and hanging doors. All that changed in early 1861, however, when South Carolina led the other southern states in seceding from the Union. Nervous Unionists in San Francisco feared that "pro-Secesh" forces might try to attack and seize the forts on the Bay.

Kentucky-born Colonel Albert Sydney Johnston was the Army's Commander of the Department of the Pacific. To head off any attempts by local Southern sympathizers to capture the Bay, Johnston ordered the garrison on newly finished Alcatraz Island to go on full alert, and directed that troops immediately occupy the nearly complete fort at Fort Point. On February 15, 1861, Company I of the Third U.S. Artillery Regiment, Captain John Lendrum commanding, moved into the unfinished quarters and empty gun casemates of the fort.

The soldiers' first orders reflected Johnston's overriding concern that the fort might be attacked momentarily by Southern sympathizers—the greatest perceived threat was from land, not sea. Captain Lendrum was directed to keep two guards on duty at all times; none of the magazines or outer doors were to be opened without an officer present; a patrol was to search the perimeter of the fort within distance of rifle shot before the sallyport was opened; and the entire garrison was to be kept under arms while the patrol was outside the fort.

The artillerymen of Company I, however, were the keepers of a fort without cannon — a "toothless tiger." The fort would not receive its guns for the casemates or barbettes for nearly three months. Pro-secessionists boasted that they could easily capture the fort, so when the first guns arrived the artillerymen mounted them on the barbette tier of the gorge, facing south to repel a land attack rather

In 1857, a visiting reporter for the Daily Alta California was astonished by both the sheer quantity of brick and granite and the exceptional quality of workmanship at the fort: "solid masonry of more than ordinary artistic skill which meets the eye at every point, and the visitor is at a loss to determine what he admires most—the granite or the brickwork . . . . calculated to reflect the greatest credit on the skill of those who fashioned it . . . . The fort is destined to be the cynosure of all who take pride in the dignity of labor and the advance of art. We cannot do justice to the subject in an ephemeral article. We venture to predict it will be the admiration and pride of the Pacific."

than seaward to fend off an enemy fleet. By October, additional guns had arrived and the annual ordnance report showed 55 guns mounted inside the fort, mostly on the first tier and atop the barbette.

Colonel Johnston resigned his command on April 13, 1861, the day following the attack on Fort Sumter. His replacement, General Edwin Sumner, posted new orders upon receiving word of the outbreak of war. The Bay's two forts were to be ready for instant action, and all ships entering the harbor were to be inspected by a revenue cutter and their intentions verified before being allowed to moor along the waterfront. If any vessels were spotted flying the rebel flag, they were to be immediately stopped or "fired into and sunk."

No Confederate ships ever tried to run the gauntlet of defenses that sprang up around San Francisco Bay during the Civil War. The artillerymen—over 500 in June 1865—occupied the fort mainly as an armed deterrent at the Golden Gate. Soldiers were frequently moved in and out of the fort, and during the presidential election of 1864 the troops were sent into San Francisco to provide additional security against possible rioting.

The closest the fort ever came to seeing combat actually occurred after the end of the Civil War. In the summer of 1865, news reached San Francisco that the Confederate raider *Shenandoah* was off the California coast. The ship's commander, Captain James Waddell, had been at sea for over a year and was unaware that the Confederacy had fallen. Waddell's plan was to run past Fort Point at night, ram and disable the Navy's picket ship, and turn his guns on San Francisco. Artillerymen at Fort Point and Alcatraz were ready, but they waited in vain for the *Shenandoah*. Only a few days away from the Golden Gate, Waddell learned from a friendly British ship of the peace at Appomattox Court House and dropped his plan to capture San Francisco.

Life at Fort Point

Throughout the Civil War, the soldiers at Fort Point waited for an enemy that never came. For most of the war, life at the fort was a never-ending series of drills, parades, gun practice and maintenance work. Every day, soldiers responded to a seemingly endless succession of bugle calls and drum rolls interrupted by periodic inspections by visiting dignitaries and weekly artillery exercises.

The population of the fort fluctuated throughout the 1860s, with some companies spending only a few weeks at the post. The longest stay at the fort is credited to Company B of the Third Artillery, which arrived in March 1861 and stayed for the next two and a half years.

As a post, Fort Point was damp, cold, and isolated. The fort was on a tip of land of great strategic value but it was frequently enveloped in fog and swept by strong winds. Spray from crashing Pacific waves often blew over the parapet walls of the barbette tier, making life miserable for the sentries on duty. The interior courtyard of the fort was arranged like a well, and for much of the day the parade ground and living quarters were cloaked in deep shadows. The thick walls of the fort, designed to keep out enemy artillery fire, created dank living quarters. The only heat came from tiny fireplaces in each of the gorge rooms, and it took hours for a smoky coal fire to heat up the interior of a gloomy casemate.

Garrison life was considerably better for the officers assigned to the fort than for the enlisted soldiers. The second tier of the gorge was "officers' country," where unmarried officers were assigned individual bedrooms. Each pair of bedrooms shared a common parlor, and personal furnishings for these rooms were popular; a well-turned-out parlor might feature curtains, carpets, a hooked rug, paintings on the walls and damask-covered chairs. A few lucky officers were allowed to bring their wives to the post, and before the end of the Civil War a handful of woodframe residences were built south of the fort for these married officers. Officers were also part of San

Francisco's privileged class of society, and invitations to dress balls, parties and other events offered pleasant breaks from the monotony of duty in a seacoast fortress.

Enlisted men enjoyed few luxuries at Fort Point. Living in the third-tier gorge casemates, the privates and non-commissioned soldiers lacked almost all of the comforts enjoyed by the officers downstairs. The enlisted men slept in two-man bunks, twelve bunks to a casemate, twenty-four men to a room filled with the mingled aromas of sour straw, stale tobacco and unwashed, wet woolen uniforms. A soldier had few possessions, restricted to what could be stuffed in a pack stowed at the foot of the bunk or hung on a wooden wall peg. Mattresses were sacks filled with straw ticking, the latrine was at the end of the tier and personal hygiene was basic. (Army regulations stipulated mandatory bathing once a week and washing of the feet twice a week.)

Defense Against the Sea: The Seawall

Almost as soon as the soldiers moved into the new fort they found it was literally being eaten away by natural forces. When the bluff of Cantil Blanco was demolished to make way for the new fort, its rocky remains were spread along the shore to protect the new fortification's foundations. By early 1862, though, much of this rubble had eroded and waves were threatening to undermine the concrete and granite footings. Engineers began to focus their attentions on construction of a seawall to protect the fort.

Over the next eight years, work progressed on a 1,500-foot granite seawall enclosing the tip of Fort Point that would have to withstand the full force of the Pacific Ocean. Thousands of tons of granite blocks were imported from Folsom, California, and laid together in interlocking keyed courses backed with concrete and packed rubble. The spaces between the stones were filled with cement, then covered with tar-impregnated cloth and molten lead to keep out the salt water. The seawall was finally completed in 1869, just as soldiers began vacating the fort.

The new seawall, a masterpiece of engineering, protected a fortress whose day was rapidly passing. Military engineers had studied the performance of forts similar to Fort Point during the Civil War and came up with a dismal forecast: advances in modern long-range rifled artillery made these masonry forts obsolete. The most notable example of a failed casemated work occurred at Fort Pulaski near Savannah, Georgia, where Union guns demolished the fort's seven-foot thick walls in just under 48 hours. Now that the war was over, the U.S. Army was having serious doubts about the wisdom of protecting the country's crucial harbors with such vulnerable targets.

Recreation

Common soldiers had few choices for recreation at Fort Point. Fishing off the seawall was a frequent diversion, as were the concerts put on by the Presidio band. Although gambling was prohibited, checkers and dominos were popular, along with clandestine games of poker and three-card monte. Fleshier diversions were available to men willing to hike the hills to San Francisco's waterfront and visit the saloons along what was becoming known as the Barbary Coast.

The artillerymen at Fort Point left in March 1868. Where only four years before the fort had been reported "in perfect order and cleanliness," an inspection of the post a few months after closing revealed a dismal picture. The guns were badly cared for, their wooden carriages were in disrepair, ironwork around the gun embrasures was rusting, the interiors of the barracks rooms were falling apart, and several unmounted guns were found lying in the surf near the fort's wharf. The reporting officer was furious: "There must be something wrong in a military organization which can present such carelessness."

THE FORT AT FORT POINT, he concluded, "was sadly in want of a commanding officer." As it turned out, the fort would be in want of a good commanding officer—and a garrison—for another ten years.

Fort Point's seawall withstood thundering Pacific waves for over one hundred and twenty years. By the 1980s, however, the wall was undermined. Huge boulders placed in front of the seawall's granite face now help slow the erosion.

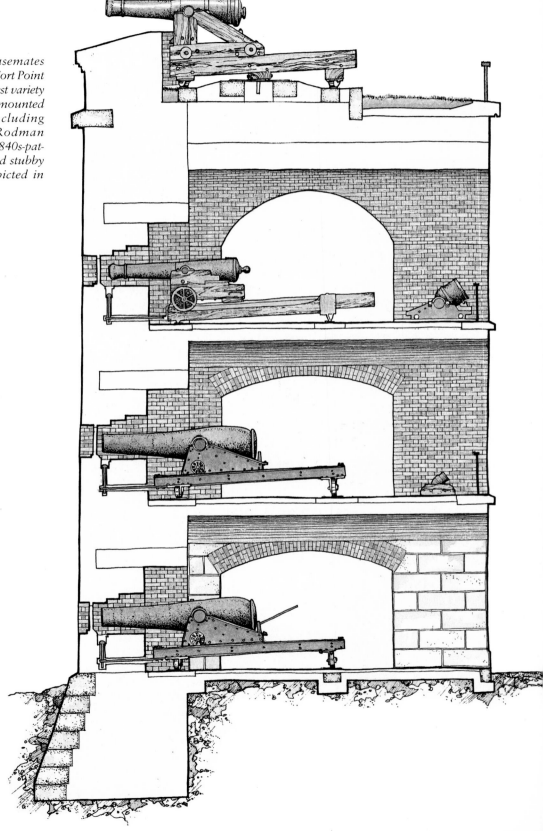

In 1869, the casemates and barbette of Fort Point housed the greatest variety of cannon ever mounted in the fort, including streamlined Rodman guns, obsolete 1840s-pattern cannon, and stubby mortars, as depicted in this illustration.

The Guns of Fort Point

Although Fort Point was never totally armed (few Third System forts were), the fort still bristled with an impressive array of 19th-century ordnance. Cannon during the 19th century were generally classified according to the diameter of their bores or the weight of the cannonballs they fired. The guns at Fort Point and its detached batteries ranged in size from relatively small 24-pounder guns up through 10-inch caliber "Columbiad" guns and the monstrously large 15-inch "Rodman" guns.

Cannon of the Early 1860s

Fort Point's smallest guns were mounted in the lower tiers of casemates during the fort's initial period of armament. By late October 1861, when the first annual ordnance report was filed, the first tier held 28 of the 42-pounder guns facing the channel, along with two 24-pounder guns in the east bastion aiming back down the approach road to protect the land side of the fort. The second tier was empty except for two 24-pounders in the east bastion facing the road. The third tier was also vacant except for a pair of 24-pounders. The barbette sported the greatest variety of ordnance; eleven 32-pounders faced the hill south of the fort, eight 8-inch Columbiads lined the main channel face, and two 10-inch Columbiads flanked the line of 8-inchers. Outside the fort's walls, four more 24-pounders were emplaced in the counterscarp gallery and ten 42-pounders were mounted in the Ten Gun Battery on the hill.

Grape Shot

The 24-pounder and 32-pounder guns, although capable of using shot and shell, generally fired either canister or grape shot. These murderous loads consisted of clusters of small balls which sprayed out of the cannon's muzzle with a devastating, shotgun-like effect. Canister and grape would most surely have been used against any troops assaulting Fort Point.

Hot Shot

Perhaps the oddest type of projectile available to Civil War gunners was "hot shot." Two furnaces once stood in Fort Point's parade where solid cannonballs could be heated until cherry-red. The hot shot were then quickly loaded into one of the first tier's 42-pounders and fired. When the red-hot cannonball hit a wooden ship, it would bury itself in the hull and set the vessel afire. Surprisingly, hot shot could be ricocheted across wave tops without cooling off. Skipping the cannonballs across the Bay was the accepted method of using hot shot.

The fort's main powder magazine was a labyrinth of wooden racks and carefully stowed powder kegs. The gunpowder tended to separate during long storage, so soldiers routinely removed the kegs and rolled them around to re-mix the contents.

Artillery Practice

The main purpose of Fort Point's existence was the defense of the Golden Gate, and the mission of the soldiers stationed there was to service the guns of the fort. Weekly artillery practice was held throughout the Civil War years, and the public was often invited to watch the proceedings. The fort's biggest guns were five-ton behemoths known as "Columbiads," capable of firing either a solid shot or an explosive shell nearly two miles. It took great strength to load and aim the guns, and a crew that could get off two aimed shots in five minutes was rated top notch.

In the years of black powder and cast-iron cannon, artillerymen faced a hazardous job. The titanic moving masses of cannon and gun carriages took a heavy toll on human flesh. The irregularities of casting techniques used in the early guns led to the constant fear of accidental bursts during artillery practice. (In 1861, a Columbiad on Alcatraz Island split open during target practice, wrecking the gun carriages on either side.) The notoriously loud concussion when the big guns fired was deafening, and in the casemates the sound could burst eardrums. Soldiers commonly complained of profuse bleeding from their noses and ears after extended target practice.

Rodmans and Rifled Muzzle Loaders

Beginning in 1868, new guns of an 1861 model known as "Rodmans" were installed in many of the fort's casemates. More sleek than the earlier-pattern cannon mounted during the Civil War, these guns reflected the improved casting techniques of American foundries.

Many of the Rodmans were 10-inch smoothbores, but a number of these guns had been altered by inserting 8-inch rifled sleeves into their barrels, earning them the name "Rifled Muzzle Loaders." Rifled guns of this pattern had much greater accuracy than smoothbores of the same caliber. However, since no artillerymen were stationed at the fort to fire the new guns, all of this advantage went to waste; the new Rodmans were mostly used for training by visiting troops.

Obsolete Armament

In 1881, Fort Point housed 102 guns, the greatest number of cannon ever mounted in its defenses. Ironically, most of these artillery pieces were pre-Civil War models already condemned as obsolete, and starting in 1885 the guns began to be removed. Although Fort Point was barely twenty years old, most of its armament was only fit for use as ornaments on parade grounds or for sale as low-grade scrap.

Shots and Shells

Each of Fort Point's guns was designed to fire a variety of destructive projectiles. The simplest type of cannonball was a solid, round iron ball called a "shot," but most of the fort's guns were designed to also fire hollow explosive balls called "shells." Shells were fitted with slow-burning fuses, timed to detonate just as they hit the target, and were much preferred by gunners for shattering ships' rigging or clearing decks of sailors.

Pioneer photographer Eadweard Muybridge documented the empty fort in 1870. A line of Columbiad guns points toward the Golden Gate, while in the foreground a child lounges on a 32-pounder gun with its stands of grape shot.

§

The Fort Becomes a Barracks
1868 – 1914

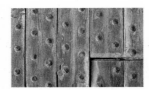

THE YEARS FOLLOWING 1868 were lonely ones at Fort Point. No soldiers were posted there for nearly ten years, and the fort was relegated to caretaker status. The little work that did take place focused on completing the seawall and fighting the on-going battle against rust. While the war had shown how vulnerable casemated forts could be, engineers weren't ready to give up on what had become known to locals as "old Fort Point." Instead, they looked for ways to adapt the work to meet the challenge of rifled artillery.

Beginning in 1870, workers began erecting batteries of a radically different style along the slopes above the old fort. Constructed of masses of dirt and masonry, the new "earthwork" gun emplacements of Batteries East and West (so-named because of their locations to the east and west of the old fort) soon began stretching along the heights of the Presidio. Designed to mount 15-inch caliber Rodman guns, the earthworks would serve as a simple, inexpensive defense that could easily be adapted to more modern gun designs.

In 1876, however, all worked ceased at Fort Point when Congress refused to allocate money for construction of America's coastal defenses. Even the earthwork Batteries East and West stood incomplete, with only a handful of their 15-inch guns in place.

The fort's caretaker, officially titled the Fort Keeper, now found himself not only combating rusty iron in the old fort but fighting off the advancing hordes of gophers which multiplied in the slopes of the earthwork batteries.

Fort Point received a garrison again in 1878 when two companies of the 4th Artillery moved into the casemates. Over the next eight years, artillery and infantry soldiers would inhabit the old fort for short periods, using it primarily as a barracks rather than as a functioning defensive work.

The soldiers periodically practiced with the rifled guns mounted in the casemates of the fort and with the 15-inch smooth-bores in Battery West, but contemporary accounts reveal that accuracy was very poor. The problem apparently was with the training of the

Following the Civil War, which had shown that casemated forts like Fort Point were vulnerable to modern guns, the Army dictated that future defensive works be built of vast masses of earth and dirt, like Battery East, above. Typical of these simple earthwork fortifications, Battery East mounted 15-inch Rodman cannons. By 1876, however, all work stopped on coastal fortifications, and many, including Fort Point, eventually became barracks.

Millions of bricks went into the building of the fort. To construct the arched casemates, laborers first erected temporary wooden forms. Masons next laid brick atop the forms in interlocking patterns. The wood forms then were stripped away, the excess mortar was trimmed off, and the brick arches were planed smooth.

One of the three free
standing granite stair
ways in the fort i
another example of th
mason's art. Each ma
sive step is almost com
pletely self-supporting
extending only a fer
inches into the brick wa
of the stairwell and care
fully balanced betweei
the treads above an
below.

soldiers; the post-war budget for artillery practice was so small that the guns were only allotted an average of one shot per month. Besides, necessary maintenance had been deferred and the guns had an alarming habit of dismounting themselves during target practice. On one occasion, a 15-inch Rodman weighing 50,000 pounds jumped off its carriage in Battery West, in front of a horrified assemblage of military officers, invited dignitaries and newspaper reporters.

After only eight years the soldiers were again withdrawn, and in 1886 the fort was once more left to the care of a Fort Keeper. Thanks to its scenic location, though, the now-vacant fortress became something of a tourist attraction. A constant stream of visitors found their way into the fort. The view from the barbette tier was spectacular, and the aging Columbiad guns sitting on their platforms made favorite backdrops for photographers.

In the early 1890s, Congress made funds available for yet another generation of fortifications, and plans were drawn up for a network of modern gun batteries on both sides of the Golden Gate. Preliminary concepts called for partly demolishing the old brick fort and placing two huge 16-inch caliber rifles in its remains.

On July 13, 1890, on the eve of constructing the new concrete batteries at Fort Point, the *San Francisco Examiner* sent a reporter out to take what might have been a last look at the fort which "for many years has stood guard at the entrance to the Golden Gate." The picture he painted was evocative of an age long gone, even though the fort was less than thirty years old: "The ponderous smoothbores, once the pride of the military, are becoming rusted from want of use and the portholes are covered with cobwebs, and the grim-looking corridors which once knew the martial tread are now silent and deserted save for the merry prattle of children's voices or the presence of curious sightseers."

In 1882, one San Francisco magazine took a jaundiced view of the artillerymen's skills at Fort Point. Limited training for the soldiers, combined with poor gun maintenance and antique ammunition, resulted in embarrassing target-practice scores.

The fort had begun to lose its "teeth" by this time. The oldest cannons still in place—the pre-Civil War 42-pounder guns now mounted in the third-tier casemates—were the first ones removed in 1885. The following year the barbette was disarmed, and throughout the 1890s, the removal of obsolete ordnance continued with the scrapping of the slightly more modern 10-inch smoothbore and 8-inch rifled Rodman guns. Shortly after the turn of the century, the remaining guns were dragged out the sallyport and turned over to a scrap dealer.

Despite being disarmed, Fort Point was spared the fate of being demolished for another gun battery. By the time construction of the new fortifications began in 1892, plans for the two 16-inch guns atop the fort had been dropped. The engineers decided to leave the fort intact for the time being. It would serve well as barracks for soldiers manning the new gun batteries being erected on the site of Battery West. Shortly after the turn of the century, soldiers from the 66th Company of the newly named Coast Artillery Corps took up residence in the fort.

The Great Quake of 1906

The Great San Francisco Earthquake of 1906 found several dozen men of the 66th Company asleep in their quarters in the gorge barracks. Jolted awake by the shock of the quake, the artillerymen quickly evacuated the fort but noticed one soldier was missing. Returning to their quarters, they heard a noise coming from outside the windows where one of their men was trapped. The half-awake soldier had attempted to climb out the window, found it barred on the outside, then turned to find the window had slammed shut behind him.

The stranded artilleryman turned out to be only slightly shaken and dirty. The fort had fared much worse. A rock slide had closed the road leading to the city, the footbridge from the lighthouse keepers' residences to the top of the fort had collapsed, and perhaps most alarming, the entire gorge face had pulled away from the rest of the fort, leaving an eight-inch gap between the interior and exterior walls.

The soldiers, fearing another quake might hit at any minute, formed a human chain into the fort and passed out their clothes and personal belongings. Making their way over the rock slide into the city, they spent the next several days fighting fires and helping with relief efforts.

A formal inspection of the old fort eventually followed and the engineers decided that the cost of repairing the damaged south wall was simply too high. Fort Point was abandoned and its troops moved into new barracks south of the point. For the next several years, the fort slid deeper and deeper into disrepair, its interior slowly succumbing to the ravages of the elements and the vandalism of visitors. Despite periodic suggestions that the fort be rehabilitated for uses such as married enlisted men's quarters or as a military museum for the upcoming 1915 World's Fair, no preservation efforts took place other than an occasional sweeping out of accumulated debris.

While the Army was concerning itself with how to deal with the flood of visitors the 1915 World's Fair would draw, another government agency was making plans on how to handle the huge numbers of new immigrants that would arrive in San Francisco once the new Panama Canal opened. The Bureau of Immigration and Naturalization eventually chose Alcatraz Island as the best possible location for a new immigration station.

The fort on Alcatraz was also obsolete, and since 1907 the Army had transformed the island into a major military prison. In 1912 they had completed the world's largest concrete prison building atop the island, and it was this brand-new facility that attracted the Bureau of Immigration's attention. In 1914, two bills were introduced in Congress directing that the island be transferred to the Bureau of Immigration, and that the military prisoners be moved into old Fort Point.

What followed was one of the most intriguing and depressing chapters in the history of the fort. Before either bill ever left committee, the Army undertook the complete remodeling of Fort Point for use as a "detention barracks," committing thousands of dollars to the conversion work without ever receiving direct orders or monetary authorization from the Congress.

Throughout 1914, inmate crews from Alcatraz were ferried out to Fort Point to carry out the remodeling work. The convict workers tore up rusty gun rails, demolished the shot furnaces, paved the parade and barbette with concrete, installed toilets in the bastions, ripped out interior walls to make way for guards' barracks, cut oversized window openings into the gorge, and built wooden partitions in the casemates, dividing the gun rooms into oversized cells. The original wooden floors in the officers' and enlisted barracks were repaired, innumerable coal stoves were installed to provide heat, and the ornamental iron railings in the rear openings of the gun casemates were ripped out and replaced with wooden walls.

DESPITE ALL THE CHANGES, Fort Point never became a detention barracks. Neither congressional bill authorizing the transfer of Alcatraz was ever enacted, and the entire matter died in committee before a single prisoner ever took up residence in the fort. Perhaps the only positive result of the conversion work was the repair of the south wall; the engineers installed steel tie-rods and turnbuckles to pull the earthquake-damaged gorge face back into an upright position. From the exterior, at least, the fort still looked much as it had in the 1860s.

Fort Winfield Scott, Alias Fort Point

The old fort finally received a formal name on November 25, 1882, when the War Department issued a general order stating: "by direction of the President, the military post on the south side of the Golden Gate, California, now known as 'Fort Point,' shall hereafter be known and designated as Fort Winfield Scott." Named in honor of one of the Army's most respected 19th-century commanders-in-chief, the newly named post included both the brick fort itself and the various outbuildings and earthwork batteries that had sprouted around the northern tip of the Presidio. The name "Fort Scott" never really took hold at the old masonry fortress, though, and the building would popularly be known as "Fort Point" for the rest of its history.

In 1935, the concrete and steel webbing of the Golden Gate Bridge began to envelop the old fort, above. A maze of temporary wooden scaffolding took shape just south of Fort Point, marking the site of the bridge's southern anchorage. Inside the casemates, right, a cafeteria was set up for construction workers.

$

The Golden Gate Bridge & World War II:
1915 – 1947

ALTHOUGH THE FORT NEVER HOUSED a detention barracks, the newly rehabilitated structure served a variety of other Presidio uses. Unmarried officers moved into the gorge during the World War I troop buildup, and in the early 1920s, trade schools at the Presidio used the casemates for classrooms and shop space. The Coast Artillery also found a new use for the fort by maintaining two "base end stations" atop the barbette as range-finding positions for the latest generation of Fort Scott gun batteries. The artillerymen also installed a 60-inch searchlight on the barbette and a generator plant in the first-floor casemates.

By 1926 the fort was abandoned once again and vandals were finding their way into the structure. An inspection that year reported nearly all windows broken, ironwork badly rusting, one of the sallyport doors lying unhinged, filthy interior rooms covered with obscene graffiti, and lower-tier embrasures standing open, allowing unlimited access to tourists. The War Department, strapped for funds, spent a total of $40.37 to board up doors and windows in an unsuccessful effort to keep out intruders.

At the same time the Army was spending tens of dollars on sealing the fort, the newly created Golden Gate Bridge District was raising tens of millions of dollars through bond sales for a bridge that would span the Golden Gate from Fort Point to Lime Point. Chief Engineer Joseph Strauss initially concluded that Fort Point sat on the optimal location for a huge concrete caisson anchoring the bridge's San Francisco end. After touring the empty fort, however, he changed his mind. In a 1937 memorandum to the bridge's Board of Directors, Strauss wrote: "While the old fort has no military value now, it remains nevertheless a fine example of the mason's art. Many urged the razing of this venerable structure to make way for modern progress. In the writer's view it should be preserved and restored as a national monument. . ."

Strauss made some additional calculations and concluded that the fort could be spared by moving the southern anchorage several hundred feet south. However, in order to make up the difference in the total length, he would have to add a 'bridge within the bridge,' and consequently designed a steel arch in the southern anchorage to span the old fort. Fort Point would be overshadowed by the new bridge, but it would be preserved.

Work on the Golden Gate Bridge began in 1933. Fort Point's casemates made convenient work space for the hundreds of workers and artisans who soon swarmed around the bridge's southern anchorage, and draftsmen set up shop in the old barracks. The second-tier gun rooms served as a cafeteria for bridge workers, and atop the fort dozens of steel plates were painted with a variety of paint coatings and tints, then studied for resistance to salt corrosion. The fort was soon enveloped in a maze of wooden scaffolding as the huge steel arch was erected over the barbette tier.

Although the main casemated portion of Fort Point was spared during construction, some of the outworks of the fort had to be demolished to make way for the southern bridge anchorage. Early in the excavation process, the bluff south of the fort was cut back several hundred feet, destroying the counterscarp gallery and ten-gun battery. Bridge excavators also uncovered a long-buried adobe shed believed to be a powder magazine from the Castillo de San Joaquin. After its location was noted and photographed, the hut was demolished; it stood in a location too critical for it to be preserved.

But the bridge crews went to extraordinary lengths to preserve one of the fort's most outstanding examples of military engineering, the granite seawall. A tall concrete bridge pylon was planned for the north side of the fort, directly atop the seawall. Instead of demolishing the wall or burying it with concrete, Strauss had it dismantled, stored, and re-erected once the pylon was finished.

The Golden Gate Bridge's grand dedication took place in May of 1937. For the next few years the fort was nearly forgotten, overshadowed by the soaring new steel bridge overhead.

World War II

The outbreak of World War II brought a massive increase in military activity around the Bay. In response to the fear that Japanese submarines might try to enter the harbor, a steel net was strung across the Golden Gate in early 1942. Stretching from Sausalito to the Marina Green, the submarine net was supported by dozens of buoys. A Navy tug boat was stationed midway along the net to pull it open for allied shipping, then close it once the vessels were safely through. The net was backed up by three mine fields in the approaches to the harbor, and the mine fields in turn were guarded by small, rapid-fire gun batteries on both sides of the Golden Gate.

The Army needed a few more guns on the San Francisco side of the Golden Gate, so early in the war a pair of 3-inch caliber Anti-Motor Torpedo Boat (AMTB) guns from Marin County's forts were moved to the barbette tier of Fort Point. Named "Battery Point," the guns were positioned to protect the mine fields and submarine net from enemy ships. The AMTB guns were manned by soldiers from Battery N of the 6th U.S. Coast Artillery, who took up residence in the gorge barracks.

The interior of the fort was refurbished one more time for living quarters and office space for a new garrison. The gun casemates were remodeled into a messhall, recreation room, barber shop and post exchange, while the first-floor gorge rooms provided storage space for camouflage materials used in disguising nearby gun emplacements. By late 1944, however, the threat of Japanese attack had disappeared and the Fort Point troops were removed.

THE RAPID DEMOBILIZATION following the end of the war left the Army with little time or money for preservation of the again-vacant fort. The few visitors who did find their way to the boarded-up structure found a desolate scene. The sallyport doors were kept locked, and only furtive glimpses of the interior were visible through chinks in concrete cinderblocks plugging the lowest tier of embrasures. The railings along the seawall had long-since rusted away, and generations of fishermen had dug most of the lead sheathing from between the granite blocks for use as sinkers. Even the three old lighthouse keepers' houses stood vacant, the Army unable to find anyone willing either to live beneath the incessant noise of the bridge or able to put up with the perils of debris dropped by pedestrians on its sidewalks.

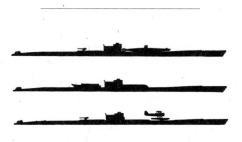

Submarine Net
By late 1944, the threat of Japanese attack had nearly disappeared, and the Fort Point troops were removed. A persistent local story maintains that the submarine net was also removed about this time and shipped to a naval base in the far Pacific, but that the Army didn't want to alert any possible enemy observers. Instead, the story goes, the tug and its string of flotation buoys were left behind to go through the motions of opening and closing a non-existent submarine net each time a ship went by.

Lighthouses at Fort Point

Fort Point may have set a record for lighthouse construction; the site featured three different lighthouses within ten years, one of which gained notoriety for being razed before it ever showed a light.

The U.S. Lighthouse Board decided to erect a light at the point in 1852 as an aid to ships entering the harbor during the Gold Rush. The Board ordered a combination keepers' residence and tower built at the tip of Punta Del Cantil Blanco, and before the end of 1852 a Cape Cod style lighthouse had been erected atop the point. The completed lighthouse awaited only the arrival of its brass-bound crystal lens to go into service.

Unknown to the Lighthouse Board, the Army Corps of Engineers also had plans for Cantil Blanco — they intended to cut it down to water level for their new casemated fort. In mid-1853 the old Spanish fort, the promontory on which it stood, and the brand new lighthouse were torn down. The engineers quickly worked out an arrangement with the Lighthouse Board to build another light tower just north of the fort at the Army's expense.

The second light structure was completed in early 1855 and began operation March 21st. Its lantern was classified as a fifth-order Fresnel-pattern lens, producing a magnified beam of light visible twelve miles at sea.

The two light keepers, or "wickies" as they were familiarly known, were responsible for both operating the light and for winding up the counterweights on an 1,100-pound fog bell mounted just outside the fort's walls. Local mariners, though, claimed the light was too dim for such an important location.

The two assistant keepers' houses at the Fort Point Light Station were built atop the hill south of the fort. A windlass helped haul supplies up the steep slope to the "wickies" homes. Terra cotta pipes in the foreground were for plumbing.

The lighthouse soon had more severe problems than complaints from seafarers; the very land the tower sat on was being washed away by Pacific storms. In 1863, while the Army planned to build a granite seawall to protect the foundations of Fort Point, the Lighthouse Board secured permission to relocate the tower to the barbette tier of the fort itself.

The third lighthouse, a nine-sided iron tower mounted atop one of the fort's spiral staircases, went into operation in January 1864. The Fort Point Light Station soon became known as one of the more desirable billets for West Coast wickies. The duties were relatively easy, the view inspiring, and the pleasures of San Francisco nearly unlimited. (This last benefit was greatly appreciated by men who had served at remote stations such as Pt. Reyes, where several 19th-century keepers were hauled away after going insane.)

The Fort Point staff eventually increased to three keepers, and modern improvements such as electricity and a compressed-air foghorn made life easier for the crew. The wickies also found themselves carrying out duties more closely associated with tour guides and lifeguards than lighthouse keepers. The crowds that visited the point always seemed to find some new way to wriggle their way into the abandoned fortress, and tourists unfamiliar with the hazards of "sneaker" waves rolling in from the Pacific regularly ended up in the waters of the Gate. Keeper James Rankin set a record by rescuing eighteen people from the frigid waters of San Francisco Bay during his 41 years at Fort Point.

The early 1930s brought the end of the Fort Point Station. The rising towers and anchorages of the Golden Gate Bridge that overshadowed old Fort Point also blotted out the light shining from its stubby lighthouse tower. In 1934 the station was shut down and its last keepers transferred to other lights, their duties assumed by an automatic lighthouse at the foot of the south bridge tower and remotely controlled fog signals along the span.

Restoring Fort Point:
1947 – Present

P U B L I C   C U R I O S I T Y   A B O U T   F O R T   P O I N T   increased after World War II, and in 1947 a reporter doing a piece on the abandoned fort queried an Army public affairs officer on the military's neglect of the seldom-seen fortress. The officer responded that while the post-war Army did not have funds to rehabilitate the fort, the War Department "might be amenable to its conversion to a public monument."

The idea of preserving Fort Point purely for its historic and architectural value had its origins in 1926. In that year, the prestigious American Institute of Architects (AIA) had written Secretary of War Dwight Davis about the deterioration of the fort. The AIA urged the Secretary to implement necessary repairs and begin routine maintenance of Fort Point, and to remove the "temporary partitions which alter the original historical purpose of the (fort's) plan."

Following World War II, a movement took hold to protect and preserve Fort Point. In March 1947, the Army hosted an "open house" at the fort commemorating 100 years of U.S. military presence on the site. General Mark Clark, Commanding Officer of the Sixth Army, proposed to declare the fort surplus and turn it over to the War Assets Administration for disposal to an agency that might preserve it as a public attraction.

A partly demolished wall in the main powder magazine is preserved as a reminder of the alterations carried out during the 1914 conversion of the fort to a detention barracks that was never completed.

Since the fort sat on federal land, the National Park Service (NPS) was the most likely candidate to receive the fort. If the NPS didn't have the funds, the State of California seemed the next most probable recipient. But that didn't stop other preservation-minded groups from making a bid for control of the fort. The hoped-for transfer never took place—a War Department study determined, somewhat surprisingly, that it was still in the nation's interest to retain possession of the area.

Preservation efforts languished for nearly ten years. The fort was opened only for infrequent tours and to the general public for Armed Forces Day festivities. Despite several grassroots "Save-the-Fort" movements, the fort remained largely unprotected. Estimates for its restoration steadily grew higher.

Fort Point Museum Association

In 1959, a group of retired military officers and civilian engineers banded together to form the Fort Point Museum Association. Operating with the blessing of the U.S. Army, the Association spent the next eleven years raising funds for the preservation of the fort and lobbying for its creation as a National Historic Site.

The Fort Point Museum Association realized that it must make the fort accessible to the public in order to build support for legislation of a new historic park. Working hand-in-hand with the 6th Army, the Association cleaned up the interior of the fort, erected safety barricades, sponsored special open house events, hosted school groups and civic agencies on tours of the fort, and opened the sallyport doors on weekends to ever-increasing numbers of visitors.

Fort Point National Historic Site

These public activities and lobbying efforts did not go unnoticed. In 1968, local congressmen introduced bills calling for the creation of Fort Point National Historic Site. Both bills passed the House and Senate. On October 16, 1970, the bill in its final form was signed into law by President Richard Nixon.

One of the most important tasks in establishing a new park is finding the right people to manage the place. One of the first employees hired at the new Historic Site was Charles Hawkins, a retired master sergeant who had worked both for the Presidio Public Affairs Office and the Fort Point Museum Association. A veteran of the Battle of the Bulge, Charlie was hewn out of the same stuff as the sergeants who had once blustered orders at recruits on the fort's parade ground. He soon had the fort running on a tight schedule. The doors were open on a regular basis, school children toured the echoing corridors, and rangers were issued reproduction 1861 uniforms to add an air of color and authenticity to the park's interpretive programs.

Before long, historians and architects were planning much-needed restorations. Within three years of legislation, work began on the long-neglected structure, and dramatic changes quickly took place. Iron balustrades and columns were sandblasted and repainted, all the ornamental ironwork railings along the barbette tier and across the casemate and gorge faces were reproduced, the 1864 lighthouse was totally rebuilt, and historic cannon identical to those originally mounted in the fort began to reappear.

Restoration and rehabilitation continued throughout the late 1970s and into the 1980s. The exterior faces of the fort were "repointed" with replacement mortar between the bricks. Plasterers refurbished many of the interior gorge rooms on the second and third tiers. Scores of reproduction powder barrels were installed in one of the first-tier magazines, and museum exhibits telling the history of the fort and the lives of its soldiers were installed on the ground floor.

Environmental Living Program

The interpretive programs offered at Fort Point became one of the most popular features of the park. In addition to presenting guided tours to the general public, the Rangers developed experimental classes such as the Environmental Living Program. During these "ELPs," school children moved into the fort for an overnight stay and the opportunity to discover firsthand what life was like for an artillery soldier in the 1860s. Their tasks involved learning how to march and carry out the manual of arms, cooking in the field, moving cannon barrels, and standing lonely guard duty on the barbette tier during the black hours of the night.

The Sutler's Store

The sutler's store was a fixture at nearly every 19th-century Army post in the United States. Today, the spirit of the old sutler's store lives on within Fort Point. Located in a first-floor casemate next to the sally-port, the current sutler's store offers reproduction artifacts, uniform items, books and educational materials for visitors. The store is operated by the nonprofit Golden Gate National Park Association and all proceeds go toward ongoing restoration and interpretation programs at Fort Point.

The sutler, a civilian merchant licensed by the Secretary of War, sold 'luxury items' that were otherwise unavailable from the fort's quartermaster. Tobacco, candy, sewing kits, civilian-manufactured clothing, canned foods, decks of cards, "penny dreadful" novels, and on occasion, alcoholic beverages, could be found on his well-stocked shelves.

The original sutler at Fort Point was E. B. Willitson, who established his store in a woodframe building outside the fort's walls. Barrels and crates of goods lined his aisles, and oil-burning lanterns hanging from the rafters burned with a yellow glow in the smokey interior. Willitson was authorized to extend credit to up to one-third of a soldier's monthly pay to anyone whose cravings exceeded his wallet's contents. However, Willitson also appeared with the paymaster on payday to settle any outstanding accounts before the soldiers were issued their $13 salaries.

Although soldiers grumbled about the high prices and occasionally shoddy merchandise, the sutler's store still served as an oasis from the regimented routine of military life. The sutler's became an off-duty gathering spot where the troops could pass a private hour around a coal-burning stove or linger over a game of checkers.

Compare the fort today — complete with restored lighthouse, iron railings, sandblasted and re-painted fluted columns and modern buildings removed from the bar-bette tier — to the photo-graph on page 29.

Iron bolts reinforced the surface of the inner doors of the sallyport to ward off ax blows of attacking enemies. The lattice-work openings provided convenient rifle slits for the defending garrison.

The Future of Fort Point

Although much has been accomplished, more remains to be done. The interior of the fort has been stabilized, but the vast procession of brick casemates and whitewashed gorge quarters stands mostly vacant. Long-range plans call for the installation of more artillery pieces in the casemates and atop the barbette to give the visitor an impression of the lines of "cast-iron behemoths" described by 19th-century tourists. Interiors of the fort's officers' quarters and enlisted barracks will be refurnished, and someday the surgeon's dispensary will be restored with its few beds and frightening array of 1860s surgical devices. Atop the barbette, the concrete paving will be removed and replanted with grass, and in the parade a shot furnace will be rebuilt. Many of the later alterations to the fort will also be preserved to tell the story of the fort's many uses after its original military role was over.

Plans for the restoration and interpretation of Fort Point are not limited to the old fort itself. The General Management Plan also calls for the rehabilitation of Battery East's earthworks and magazines high on the hill above the fort, and the installation of a Rodman cannon in one of its brick lined emplacements.

Fort Point National Historic Site is administered today as part of the 75,000-acre Golden Gate National Recreation Area (GGNRA), the country's most heavily visited national park. Fort Point sits square in the center of GGNRA, and a network of walking and hiking trails is being developed to link the fort with other historic and recreational spots within the park. A longer-range goal may result in ferry service connecting Fort Point with Alcatraz Island, the Marin Headlands, Angel Island, Fort Mason, and other sites around the Bay.

Old Fort Point, "the fort that never fired a shot in anger," still stands beneath the Golden Gate Bridge as an impressive monument to the craftsmen who labored to create an impregnable fortress at the edge of America; a monument to the preservationists who fought to save the fort from decay and demolition; and most importantly, as a monument to the artillerymen who awaited an enemy that never came.

barbette battery – battery of cannon mounted in open positions with only a short parapet wall to protect them from enemy gunfire.

barbette tier – the top tier of a fort, where cannon are mounted on exposed positions rather than in enclosed casemates.

bastion – a tower projecting out from the main body of a fort, usually with guns positioned to sweep the exterior faces of the fort.

battery – a group of cannon in a fortification. Also, a company of soldiers assigned to man the guns, as in "Battery N of the 6th Coast Artillery."

casemate – an arched, "bombproof" masonry room. Fort Point has over 100 casemates which housed cannon, living quarters, storerooms and powder magazines.

counterscarp – a wall outside the fort facing back toward the main scarp wall, and sometimes provided with its own defense.

face – a main exterior side of a fort.

gorge – the side of an enclosed fort where the living quarters, storerooms, magazines, and shops are located.

magazine – a room for storing gunpowder or projectiles.

outwork – a smaller fortification built outside the main body of a fort, such as the Ten Gun Battery and the Counterscarp Gallery at Fort Point.

ordnance – artillery pieces and the equipment used to fire or maintain them.

projectile – an object fired from a gun, such as solid shot, explosive shells, grape shot, and canister.

rifle – gun manufactured with spiral grooves cut into the interior of the barrel, designed to fire pointed projectiles.

sallyport – a protected entrance way. Fort Point's sallyport was closed off at each end with heavy, iron-studded doors. Rifle slits line its interior walls.

scarp – the outer, exposed wall of a fort.

smoothbore – gun manufactured with a smooth interior barrel, or bore, designed to fire round projectiles.

Fort Point is open every day except Thanksgiving Day, Christmas Day
and New Year's Day. For more information, call (415) 556-1693.

What to see:
Rangers clad in full Civil War uniforms lead frequent tours of the fort, but you
may also walk around on your own. You can join a tour at the bugle call, or
load a smoothbore cannon during one of the drills.
Ground floor:
On the ground floor, visit a soldier's jail cell, examine an array of historic can-
non, walk into a powder magazine, and browse a number of special exhibits
on the fort's colorful history.
Second floor:
The second floor includes the officers' quarters, kitchen and hospital rooms.
Third floor:
The third floor houses the soldiers' barracks and non-commissioned officers'
quarters.
Fourth floor:
The barbette tier on the fourth floor offers an unparalleled view of the Bay's
entrance way from directly under the Golden Gate Bridge.

What to wear:
The fort can be extremely cold and windy any day of the year, so dress warmly
and wear comfortable, flat-soled shoes.

Walks and Hikes:
Fort Point Loop
A picturesque trail runs for less than a mile roundtrip up the hillside towards
the Golden Gate Bridge through the gun emplacements and tunnels of Battery
East and back toward Fort Point.
Coastal Trail
This 12-mile hike (one-way) wends its way past coastal views, wildflowers, and
seacoast fortifications to Fort Funston. Pick up the trail up the hillside from
the Fort Point parking lot and follow the hikers' signs along the San Francisco
Headlands to Lands End and beyond.

Suggested Reading

Bearss, Edwin. Fort Point, Historic Structures Report. U. S. Department of
the Interior, National Park Service, 1973.

Hogg, Ian. The History of Fortification. New York: St. Martin's Press, Inc.
1981.

Lewis, E. R. Seacoast Fortifications of the United States. Washington,
D.C.: Smithsonian, 1968.

Ripley, Warren. Artillery and Ammunition of the Civil War. New York:
Van Nostrand Reinhold Co., 1970.

About the Author
John A. Martini is a fifth-generation San Franciscan with twenty years experience as a national park ranger. An expert about California history and military fortifications, John has written numerous articles and books about San Francisco's coastal defenses.

The Golden Gate National Park Association wishes to thank the staff of the Golden Gate National Recreation Area who helped review and produce this publication.

GGNPA PRODUCTION MANAGEMENT
CHARLES MONEY
GREG MOORE

EDITOR
NORA L. DEANS

DESIGN
NANCY E. KOC

PHOTOGRAPHY
ALL PHOTOGRAPHY BY THEA SCHRACK EXCEPT:

ROY EISENHARDT (PAGES 1, 11, 31, 41)
GGNPA ARCHIVES (PAGES 16, 21, 23, 29, 32, 37)
BARRIE ROKEACH (PAGE 5)
DAVID TISE (PAGES 14, 15, 42)

ILLUSTRATIONS
BANCROFT LIBRARY, UC BERKELEY (PAGE 10)
GGNPA ARCHIVES (PAGES 6, 27)
KAREN MONTGOMERY (PAGE 8)
LAWRENCE ORMSBY (PAGES 2, 3, 9, 14, 18)

SET IN SABON ANTIQUA ON AN APPLE MACINTOSH WITH QUARK EXPRESS 3.0

PRINTED IN HONG KONG ON RECYCLED PAPER